METROMORPHOSES

THE HUGH MacLENNAN POETRY SERIES
Editors: Allan Hepburn and Carolyn Smart

Recent titles in the series

Metromorphoses

JOHN REIBETANZ

McGill-Queen's University Press
Montreal & Kingston • London • Chicago

ISBN 978-0-2280-2091-2 (paper)
ISBN 978-0-2280-2092-9 (ePDF)
ISBN 978-0-2280-2093-6 (ePUB)

Legal deposit second quarter 2024
Bibliothèque nationale du Québec

Printed in Canada on acid-free paper that is 100% ancient forest free
(100% post-consumer recycled), processed chlorine free

Funded by the Government of Canada   Financé par le gouvernement du Canada   Canada   Conseil des arts du Canada   Canada Council for the Arts

We acknowledge the support of the Canada Council for the Arts.

Nous remercions le Conseil des arts du Canada de son soutien.

McGill-Queen's University Press in Montreal is on land which long
served as a site of meeting and exchange amongst Indigenous Peoples,
including the Haudenosaunee and Anishinabeg nations. In Kingston
it is situated on the territory of the Haudenosaunee and Anishinaabek.
We acknowledge and thank the diverse Indigenous Peoples whose
footsteps have marked these territories on which peoples of the world
now gather.

Library and Archives Canada Cataloguing in Publication

Title: Metromorphoses / John Reibetanz.

Names: Reibetanz, John, 1944- author.

Description: Series statement: The Hugh McLennan poetry
series | Poems.

Identifiers: Canadiana (print) 20230561799 | Canadiana (ebook)
20230561810 | ISBN 9780228020912 (softcover) |
ISBN 9780228020929 (ePDF) | ISBN 9780228020936 (ePUB)

Classification: LCC PS8585.E448 M482024 | DDC C811/.54—dc23

This book was typeset by Marquis Interscript in 9.5/13 Sabon.

For my children

and the city we share

real and imaginary

CONTENTS

Contents

Contents

I

SHALL WE GATHER AT THE RIVER?

They did for eleven thousand years
each generation portaging then
gliding on sky-mirroring current

to the mouth of the river that in
fall was riveted with the gleaming
armour of salmon gathering for

upstream homecomings where the river
bore a more muted burden of leaves
past smaller winter settlements and

burial sites the banks gathering
them and their prized possessions a pipe
at one through which a current of smoke

once flowed its bowl carved in the figure
of a pregnant woman her body
birthing fragrance and at another

a comb over whose teeth a horned snake
glides and forms the tail of the panther
Mishipizhew from whose head rises

a bear whose bent torso waterfalls
into a human sitting astride
the panther the same current of life

charging through their veins like a river
emptying into the sea where mists
gather and rise and return as rain.

The flow of water and the flow of words
for them were one the waterway a speech-
way both picking up images of sky

or bird on surfaces while from within
where currents chirruped over the streambed
and gutturals glided across the tongue

songnotes of wren or warbler rose to fill
the curvatures of riverbank or ear
verbs coming first in wing-spun sentences

the way an eager round of water shoots
pure energy out past the waterfall's
stone rim into an air thickened to mist

the mist an image of the nebulous
dreamworld where spirits pour discourse into
ears asleep to the noise that thinks itself

the only source of life's upwelling voice
as when the loud retort of strangers' guns
replaced the arrow's whispers and a land

figured as rivering footsteps hardened
into holdings where Pahoombwawindung
named after *the approaching roaring thunder*

froze into Thomas Smith and *the sparkling
light* of Naningahseya was dimmed down
to William Jackson the deep channel blocked

between person and place the footed and
the rooted the Don's Anishinaabe
name Wonscoteonoch appealing to

Elizabeth Simcoe's sympathetic
pale ear word giving voice to the flowing
heart of *black burnt country once swept by fire.*

UNKNOWN EARTH

1

Nobody knew it lived there just beneath
our feet a webwork of pathways that mocked
the sterile straightness of old Roman roads

a looping crisscross up-down in and out
as vital to frail-rooted tundra blooms
as to redwood forests' pillared reaches.

Networks of microscopic caves are mapped
by scientists hoping to protect them
and the deep-shelved carbon they've protected.

2

Eighteenth-century geographers mapped
terra incognita not knowing who
lived in and knew the New World's winding trails.

Joseph Bouchette surveying Toronto
in 1793 saw "trackless"
forests where feet had tracked forest-dwelling

creatures for thousands of years before his
telescopic tools replaced those of stone.
Nobody protected the pathmakers.

Did you lift your tired child up
for a shoulder ride? Is that why
the little footprint disappears
and yours stamps a moccasined heel
into the clay, to hoist the load?

Workers at the excavation
couldn't believe their eyes: footprints
on our lakebed seventy feet
beneath the surface, and heading
northwards towards the city shoreline

under the waves, a miracle
only partly less amazing
than to learn the lake was dry land
and that you set your emblem there
eleven thousand years ago.

The Golden Age of Athens waits
three times as far ahead into
your future as it slips behind
into our past in what we now
call Before the Common Era.

Common in what way? How can I,
cellphoned and supermarketed,
commune with your hieroglyphics,
follow as you stalk mastodons
or spear extinct fish from the lake

unless in the shifting shoreline
I see a future that I share
with your child, not a golden age
but a trackless expanse best met
hoisted on a father's shoulders.

1

clunk goes the archaeologist's
trowel on Local Evening News
through loam poking worked bone worked shell

worked antler till the sought-for *clink*
of shard dates this burial site
near the displaced mouth of the Don

to one thousand BCE when
the art of firing pottery
first took hold in Ontario

2

some shards bear ribbed cubes that some hand
pressed into wet clay with stone tools
some zigzag etched with a tool's edge

the hand's work surviving the hand
the art of cremation having
arrived with that of pottery

hardened clay fragments held their ground
while lime from tanning-yards and lye
from soapworks dissolved the ashes

3

if asked why give the body up
to flames the elders might recall
elders of generations back

who saw flame-zigzags from the clouds
turn trees to ash and rising from
ash as in legend fireweed

itself displaced by berry bush
that nourished bear and hare and moose
that nourished living human flesh

4

whose ashes not preserved from change
like hardened shard feed birthing soil
in underground economy

potlatch of bone exchanged for bone
antler for skull for antler in
circles of gift whose origin

those zigzags on the shards depict
a never-displaced river that
pours from the fire in the sky

THE DON RIVER'S DANCE
AT SKINNER'S MILL

Timothy Skinner was married to
a mortal but wedded to water
in a lifelong partnership of love

and hate loving water's glimmer as
it sashayed through the milldam's spillway
to power the waterwheel that sent

sawblades up and down or runner stones
spinning over the bedstone's grain where
flour poured like white water from its grooves

hating autumn days when water turned
a cold shoulder to the wheel and he
two-stepped through the millrace chipping ice

to keep wheel and driveshaft whirling clear
into the winter when all milling
stopped in water's snow-capped tracks the way

it had to in summer droughts during
water's absence but water always
came back unlike Tim who aged and went

missing forever leaving water
widowed but still dancing in silver
slippers over the milldam's polished stones.

THE MAKING OF A NATURALIST

After one of the worst beatings from my father
I got away from the house as fast as I could.

Ernest Thompson Seton

The trapshoot ran through his head as he ran
    once again over the Don flats
where the local game club released shore larks
    and redpolls from collapsible
cages so they could fly up and be shot.

Digging in his pocket for the few
    coins earned doing chores for neighbours
he'd bought two imprisoned birds and brought them
    to a forest clearing far from
trappers and guns and let them flutter free

among the tall white pines whose wind-rocked crowns
    swayed like wands of giant wizards
but housed nests snug as the dugout shanty
    in undergrowth below fox vines
that screened the banked den where he sheltered now

magicked by the woods to an "Indian"
    like those he'd read about who lived
in peace with their children and with children
    of the wild some furred some feathered
each with its own language of sound or scent

that they had learned and that he taught himself
in the schoolhouse of his shanty
reading short-lived calligraphy that was
written in gesture or printed
on the floor of his forest library

his own writing starting as a drawing
an effort to save the perfect
wings beak toes all of a dead hawk
before the maggots ran with it
a still life to hold something of life's spell.

SPECIES SONG

When he first hiked the Don Valley trails
all he heard was river as he strode
beside its glitter of smashing glass

that and the wind which sieved a thin tune
through pine needles near the crest and coaxed
applause from aspen leaves farther down

but in time wind lifted waves of sound
from sources neither flowing nor fixed
as bitterns mimicked thunder's bass drum

redpolls reloaded and then discharged
their miniature pistols of song
and larks rose on rising trill-ladders

while after sunset crickets kept warm
flicking steel sticks across steel pickets
drawing reed-notes from wakened bat throats

and making him wonder what he had
to give in return what change of breath
to music might carry not only

a lone voice but send his species song
reverberating like the others
through the valley the way a few boughs

of apple wood could transform woodshed
to orchard then he lit on whistling
which was near kin to their wordless notes

and like them would ride soundwaves over
the densest undergrowth he whistled
Beethoven up steep slopes and Mozart

ambling down Haydn on tableland
and became known as Symphony Pete
his pursed lips pouring out the shared life

II

MOSS PARK, THE HON.
WILLIAM ALLAN HOUSE

After he married Leah Gamble
William joked that she was his only
gamble and it was true he'd fared well
paying *very cautious attention*

to finances and detail ... the most
secure merchant in the town of York
waiting thirty years to build a house
on his two-hundred-acre park lot

naming it not after lofty trees
(no Oaklands not even Hazelburn)
but after the humble moss that hugged
the north side of his trees' trunks and roots.

It didn't work. After five of their
children died whooping cough claimed the twins
Leah bore months after they moved in
and an eighth child fell to consumption.

William switched his loyalty from moss
to stone commissioning a columned
portico with an enclosed front porch
too late to save another daughter.

Years passed. William paced his Moss Park grounds
reflecting how the rootless mosses
(no stone foundation for them) welcomed
the rain swelling and greening with it.

In his seventieth year his last
commission was for a tree-like web
of pipes to steep the house with water
and tap the life of the clouds like moss.

Ann must have seen him on the street
in that one year 1890
her last on earth and his first in
a cottage only steps from hers

Henry easy to recognize
Black in an Irish neighbourhood
and famous for once having mailed
himself to freedom in a box

both escapees she with Martin
from famine in the old country
and Henry from a slave's starved life
in the southern part of the new

both finding refuge on Bright Street
in workers' cottages where four
rooms and a hall were crammed into
a dim four-hundred-square-foot box

which must have reminded Henry
of the packing crate that nearly
took his life when overturned with
him clinging inside upside down

but he made a name for himself
when onstage as a magician
he climbed from it the picture of
resurrection night after night

while Ann widowed with six children
remained inside the wooden walls
to be joined by her widowed child
Mary and Mary's two children

until Ann's name left the census
like those pictures she saw in church
of Virgin Mary uncoffined
levitating up to heaven

SHOES

There were 683 shoemakers
in Toronto in 1871
and only 232 blacksmiths
proving people more than horses needed shoes.

Bridget Ann Treacy McTague's need was so great
she married a shoemaker to help her keep
her feet grounded after a nightmare childhood
in Ireland's famine and on the "coffin ship"

where aged seven she had chewed her shoelaces
partly from hunger but mostly because her
little brother Thomas vanished in the crowd
at the dockside and was never seen again

although even through old age she could hear him
clomping up the gangplank in dreams where her ship
had pulled away from the dock and rode the waves
that carried her out of earshot from his cries.

In Toronto like a deck the floor under
her feet kept shifting as the young couple kept
moving house sharing their cramped ship-like quarters
with the families of other shoemakers.

It must have comforted her in after years
as house after house vanished into the great
sea of new construction to know that she could
never lose her foothold on the solid earth.

Body stooped eyes lightless Robert Baldwin
made an odd hero even apart from
the icky matter of a post-mortem
C-Section to match that of his late wife

not to mention his mumbled speech his
retreat into early retirement
at a small cottage facing away from
the best vista in early Toronto

and periodic bouts of depression
visiting him with problems of motor
control the childish handwriting that his
political enemies ridiculed

yet if the Epistle to the Hebrews
he loved may be trusted and *faith is the*
substance of things hoped for the evidence
of things not seen his wife's faith in Robert

was matched by that of his constituents
as he campaigned successfully for bi-
lingual government (sending his four
children to francophone schools in Quebec)

for women's rights for education's doors
open to all not only to the sons
of privilege his own faith powerful
as the love that survived Eliza's death

and surfaced not only in depression
but in her letters that travelled with him
and on walks where she was felt though *not seen*
and in a heroic desire to bear

her wound with him into their afterlife.

I

The music you hear when you look at
the photo is silent like the sort
that runs through the heads of the bowler-
hatted mustachioed men standing

at the wooden racks of what once was
the music hall of the Mechanics'
Institute until converted to
a public library reading room

rental of the hall deemed less crucial
than reading to "liberate the mind"
along with lectures on everything
from physics to ancient history.

Frescoed Muses in the domed ceiling
nod their approval understanding
the magic of converting black marks
on white leaf-like pages into songs

they hear when listening in on those
liberated minds vowel breath-winds
and consonantal clusters of leaves
reverberating through their green grove

even though the ceiling and building
have long disappeared with the readers
who like us heard the song of the past
like the music of a photograph.

or is Homing from Work more accurate
since work is the one home Sam's body knows
twenty-four/seven as he scrubs hangs
irons eats and sleeps behind the counter

in Toronto in 1882
while his mind washes the Chinese Laundry
away sign and all and converts water
boiling in the tank to a stream bubbling

down to the coast near his Taishan village
the stick pulling shirts from the tank changed to
a rod hauling white sturgeon from the bay
the iron plying pleated cuffs a boat

nosing its way through the currents along
the gorge's steep-sided flanks their dense green
obliterating the white street beyond
his shop window winter easy for him

to escape with forehead wet with sweat from
the one-hundred-degree Fahrenheit room
body however calling him back with
ceaseless whimpers from bent spine and stretched arms

as it will do when his mind has left it
behind and his bones after seven years
in a shallow Toronto grave will be
cleaned and shipped home to the ancestral plot.

III

III

You could be standing on the opposite
bank of the Grand Canal gazing across
ripples at a row of grand *palazzi*
which is what the architects imagined

not squinting at this brown-edged photo shot
from a rowboat in Toronto Harbour
the gabled 1890s boathouses
squatting on piers that hide the railway yards.

Never mind that shifting winter ice would
sever legs from under the piers or that
summer storms would pitch warped clapboard facades
overboard what their hearts desired was

to clothe the unknown in the familiar
by a reach of the imagination
over rippled waters of time and place
the way the town's earliest surveyor

set it back in the British countryside
by penning a green common redolent
of shade and grazing sheep though steep ridges
and river gorges riddled the terrain

or the way Elizabeth Simcoe's gaze
elevated the flat peninsula
dreaming it into "Gibraltar" and wove
Iroquois blankets into highland capes

as your gaze paints colour on this photo's
black and white greening grey clapboard villas
coating their roof tiles with red sunset glow
changing the harbour into your Venice.

TORONTO VERANDAHS

Settlers retired from army service
shipped the idea with them in sea-chests
along with *bungalows* from India
where both made sense – the bonneted cottage
shielded from sun by the lace-veiled arcade

though no Canadian wants less sun
or more flat walking-space to shovel
or curlicues under the eaves
where snow can lurk and sink into
the wood unless it's painted every year

yet the Macklins insisted on
trellised arches whose wooden vines
caper and whorl like Victorian script
across the title page of the stone house
that rewarded them after a quarter-century's work

and Jesse (grandson of the widowed
Sarah Ashbridge who came here
fleeing plague with her five children)
honoured her memory sixty years later
crafting a trellised verandah on her land

while the architect John Howard
compromised his lakeside view
with shade-browed posts for a verandah
he loved so much he made it open
directly into the parlour sidling along it

so determined were they all
not to live imprisoned in
a garrison but to parley with
the spirit of the place wearing
this wood-spun sundress to face the winter wind.

GOD'S HOUSE ON EARTH

I

sends arrows heavenwards from gabled porch
to steep-pitched roof (two hands angled in prayer)
to bellcote poised rocket-like on roof-ridge
haloed by an elm-wreathed roundel of sky

but sun-blessed as the foreground footpath is
this photograph from 1895
would lack the touch of life without that man
who pedals northwards on the gravelled road

and without the church's humble timbers
the board-and-batten façade that communes
less with the heavens than with the heaven-
aspiring trunks of those dark-barked elm trees.

Christ Church Deer Park held its first services
on the feast day of the down-to-earth saint
Thomas who would believe only if he
could touch the wound the spear made in Christ's side.

The wooden church survived beside the elms
until an affluent congregation
replaced its wood with monumental stone
across the road. Now a small grassed park fills

the sunny *gore* (the old church's spearhead-
shaped site) with elms long gone where a widened
Yonge Street replacing the graveled road shoots
traffic northwards past the cemetery.

In memory of Thomas Fitches

It held a kind of immortality
by singing long after their breath had failed
notes holding on long as the keys were pressed

while yet embracing their mortality
the keyboard's keys in duet with fingers
as the pedalboard danced with their shod feet

the human voice supported from below
its register but also companioned
in its home range and canopied on high

by pipes that *spoke* at two-foot pitch sounding
like the angels carved into organ lofts
on the walls of medieval cathedrals

where organ speech needed two sets of hands
one to press keys and pull out stops and one
to pump the leather lungs of the bellows

as in the early days at St George's
before Mrs Rose the organist's wife
gifted the pipes with a water motor

that breathed until fire got the upper hand
of water and the church burned down after
a Biblical threescore and fifteen years

leaving only the tower standing in
a garden where roses open scent-stops
and ivy climbs to silent crescendos.

CLAMS

*"We have 500 people coming in here and paying their $5
each every month now," said Mr. W.S. Dinnick, the manager
of the Standard Loan Company. "This plan has solved the
problem of the workingmen's houses ... They were all as
happy as clams in their little homes."*

Toronto Star, 1907

Clam an Old English word meaning to cramp
fetter constrict or pinch as an iron
clamp squeezes together so shellfish valves
were seen to shut like a pair of pincers
Clam also slang for dollar as in five.

Some of the lots were only ten feet wide
none had water mains sewers or drains no
paved roads or sidewalks *little homes* thrown up
from boards shingles tarpapered fronts and roofs
by crews of neighbours in house-building "bees."

All happy through summer and into fall
playing soccer on the flats picnicking
on the heights picking berries in ravines
refugees from Europe's crowded slumlands
out from under shadowing tenements.

Winter gifted them with unemployment
last-hired immigrants first to be fired
a struggle to keep every $5
from being spirited off by cold winds
that carried whimpers of hungry children.

Ice on the walls of the bedrooms drove them
into the kitchen to sleep on the floor
beneath the iron mouth of a woodstove
fed with bits of coal the children picked up
along the railway tracks where passing trains

sometimes picked off slower-moving children
and when the coal ran out they fed the stove
scrap lumber furniture bedroom floorboards
bone waste from Sunday dinner roasts scraped clean
clam shells scavenged from affluent garbage.

THE JUG

She lived in it or rather in the blue
transfer pattern printed on its outside
where a pavilion in a garden reached
down to the willow-shadowed riverbank

because no trees grew on Gilead Place
only telephone poles along sidewalks
shadowed by the rows of clapboard houses
that ended in a brick factory wall

no water in sight the lake a far-off
fable hidden by lofts and railway tracks
not the jug's blue-boat-floating white expanse
that framed another tree rising behind

with clustered oranges dangling from it
the way a single orange would dangle
from her hung stocking on Christmas morning
these oranges all keeping their ripeness

long after she and the jug were consigned
to earth whose clay when shaped and smoothed could
    hold
something to look up to her own blue sky
a scene imaged imagined and most real.

Not a place a person the medical
officer of health Dr Charles Hastings
all his battles naval on landlocked seas
billowing in and out of tenements

acrid sea of polluted lake water
coursing untreated into outdoor taps
serving too many thirsting mouths except
when its northward passage was blocked with ice

seas of milk sloshing in open buckets
their whiteness hiding typhoid cells that lurked
like gunboats waiting to discharge cannons
in a fresh slaughter of the innocents

seas of backyard privies overflowing
flooding laneways where crawling toddlers played
seas of dark night soil stealthily sluiced out
to vacant lots under cover of night.

Hastings' prime weapon was the photograph
shooting light-flashes to make rolling seas
stand still and render in plain black and white
proofs of the enemy germ encampments.

After foul water succumbed to chlorine
after leaking outhouses were routed
he stood on the deck of the *Island Queen*
handing out pasteurized milk to children

bound for free summer ferry excursions
laughter displacing in his ear at last
cries of the milk-fed infant daughter lost
many years and many battles ago.

IV

THE JUNGLE

It started in the early thirties
with the ovens – no not those ovens
although they figured in the later
history of the place – these ovens

were kilns in the Don Valley Brick Works
opened after freshly baked batches
of bricks were wheeled off so that scores of
unemployed homeless men might sleep there

without courting death on the cold earth
where they had pieced together rude huts
from packing crates sheet metal cardboard
giving the Valley the nickname of

The Jungle waste ground rife with wasted
men who talked of "jungling up" dinners
over open fires near the river
whose waters slaked their thirst and bathed them

until embarrassed city fathers
bundled them off to northern work camps
and gave The Jungle back to the weeds
until sheet metal and wood returned

as housing for prisoners of war
from regions whose ovens were less kind
and more efficient than the jungles
of steel glass and concrete that covered

the higher lands beyond the Valley
and that continued to germinate
on overworked barren ground excess
waste from undergrowth of city life.

HE SLEEPS

his head pillowed on the stacked newspapers
he will heft and hawk around the corner

right arm reaching over the dark headlines
left resting on his bare right leg stretched out

on a lower step where the flexed left leg
angles groundwards through a too-big knit sock

that has collapsed above a mud-caked boot
leaning sideways like the head above it.

The photograph cannot bare what he dreams
no more than peel the cloth cap from his head

if his is not the dreamless sleep of pure
exhaustion when the mind shuts off the stream

of images the way his ear's cave-mouth
has rolled a silent stone over the flow

of traffic and let the photographer
trap the sleeper in a round-windowed box.

Another box he calls *home* will claim him
at day's end when he'll share a windowless

lean-to shed with three brothers in one bed
after a dinner that would do for one

and what he might dream has no more to do
with his papers' society columns

than with their headlines about boots marching
through a Europe that might claim his future.

THE MAKING OF A CLOWN

I really got started in a big way when
I went to Shea's in Toronto.

Red Skelton

"Did you hear the one about the paper
   that injured people yes they fell
on hard Times." The audience laughs and he
   laughs triggering an avalanche
of giggles his painted smile passageway
   to an Aladdin's Cave of mirth
     Depression at the heart of every joke
      silence at the heart of laughter.

He plays Shea's Hippodrome though he would say
   he can't play anything bigger
than a piano but really he can't
   play anything childhood years spent
not on music lessons but on hawking
   papers on street corners you sense
     depression at the heart of all his jokes
      silence at the heart of laughter.

Rootless he plays to Toronto's rootless
   his travelling circus birthright
matching their hyphenated origins
   African-Canadian Italian-
Canadian Russian- Chinese- their mask
   a giggle lest their tongues betray
     depression lurking behind every joke
      silence behind the hearty laughs.

He knows as they do that who you are is
    never singular but plural
the wife-mother-bootlegger sharing selves
    with husband-father-labourer
Willie Lump-Lump one with Freddie the Free-
    loader the role his father played
        the depressed clown's made-up face a bequest
            like the silence after laughter

in the empty theatre whose silences
    could freeze chairbacks into headstones
of his father or of his friend Marcel
    Marceau's fellow Jewish victims
the two of them preferring the silence
    of pantomime where depression
        discarding laughing masks shows its true face
            and silence brings heartfelt laughter.

ALICE'S DOOR

For Irene Vallejo

Now she could hear her name with her eyes
first "A" rising out of its tall tent
then lean broomstick lording it over
its lowly beret-bedecked cousin
trailing two little wheels one an un-
finished arc one split by an axle

but it was both her name and the name
of Alice in the book her mother
read her before she could read herself
Alice who followed the rabbit down
to a room with a tiny door that
must have had a window in it for

her to see a green space beyond it
so unlike the door to her own room
which was also the living room when
her bed turned back into a sofa
a bolted door that opened onto
the grey concrete and the black asphalt.

She swung open the still smaller door
cradled in her hands and the thin white
doors inside it that let the light through
each one covered with rows of windows
where her eyes set out on their journey
and heard the absent voices calling.

HEAVEN ON ELIZABETH STREET

Except ye ... become as little children, ye
shall not enter into the kingdom of heaven.

Matthew 18:3

To the untrained eye the playground surface
offered nothing more than a flat expanse
of black asphalt but to the watcher high
up in the crow's nest of the climber's mast

the Black Sea rippled with troughs and whitecaps
and the ship's timbers trembled as it rode
the swells to where a brick façade became
the mountain yawning over a small dock

while for the two children rolling their hoops
along its outer edge the black surface
stiffened into the turf of a racecourse
where competing horses rounded the bend

and headed into the home stretch a kind
of heaven liberating both children
from the walled meanness of their tenements
though not the Heaven that a Bible Belt

sect hoped to reach by rolling hoops to mime
the ways of children Elizabeth Street
a kingdom of this world a training ground
for muscles and for visionary eyes

to climb beyond the world's imposed limits
in their future as in our present we
look at their ground and happily conflate
this place of healing with that place of play.

V

AT THE RED LION

across from Potter's Field (the Strangers'
Burying Ground) they danced in winter
when snow covered the smaller crosses
but sleighs could glide over frozen roads.

They danced under the vaulted ceiling
of the ballroom with its fireplaces
at either end keeping warm while vaults
across the way lay cold and quiet.

They danced behind the Red Lion's sign
painted with rampant lion bright red
as the blood that danced through their young veins
beyond the Bible's dim "field of blood"

until the temperance movement stopped
the flow of dance and drink and the cost
of downtown property sent the field's
tenants to more distant souterrains.

For a time eyes danced across pages
at a bookshop in the lion's lair
until a coffee shop's brown potions
replaced the red of sign and wineglass.

Across the road a bank tower holds
the field granite columns outstripping
the vanished stones the iron handles
dancing on row after row of vaults.

METROMORPHOSES

Bernini caught the moment when Daphne
sprinted from womanhood to treehood
her toes groping for roots her fingers leaves
but his stonework could never have contained
a second alteration if she tired
of twiggy life and sought some nimbler pose

the way this city's streetscapes cast off guise
after guise innyard into church into
condo theatre to bookshop to drugstore ·
the moments of transformation stretching
to years or decades less fit for sculpting
than for the time-lapse photographer's art

if he could fix his lens on Twenty-Nine
Centre Avenue and watch the wood-frame
cottages fall as the two-storey brick
Standard Foundry Company rises to
become the Shaarei Tzedec Synagogue
whose leaded glass and Stars of David give

way to the large display windows of Pearl
Furniture which shrink to a parking lot
like films of budding flowers run backwards
until a backhoe ploughs up the asphalt
and the new provincial courthouse raises
its see-through glass façade over the site

though no photographer could live that long
unless genetic engineering can
outstrip the art of civil engineers
giving our lives the slow timescale of whales
whose hearts beat twice a minute when they dive
and stretch their moments out to centuries.

STREETCAR METAMORPHOSES

Gondolas or gazebos the early
wooden streetcars with their triple-windowed
prows floated above the bright steel canals

that kept them on track an exotic touch
for a city of Sunday-worshippers
whose fixation on the straight and narrow

meant they had to re-lay the whole network
when wider cars came in but these thin rigs'
jaunty red-rimmed white roofs like straw boaters

brought summer to slushy streets the coaches
sashaying over whirling wheels the low
running board under accordion doors

threshold to a travelling world of light
worlds away from the armour-plated trams
that beetled along postwar rails mobile

bomb shelters soon to be superseded
by the car-crazed fifties' transformation
of streetcar into pseudo-bus lacking

only rubber tires the one giveaway
that bell reluctant to become a horn
its single ding shying away from blare

pure echo asperging polluted air
with a promissory note that recalled
comforts of an earlier age a note

evoked by the rails' latest avatar
whose five articulated living rooms
cushion commuters behind lofted glass.

They carry a thin resurrection on
the glossy side where a sliver of light
captured in a black box decades ago
can raise demolished buildings along with
the now-antique cars idling beside them
where plumes of exhaust linger forever.

Their *here* can also salvage sunken ships
like the *Empress of Ireland* riding high
above her rippled reflection before
her fatal tryst with the collier *Storstad*
just as the *here* restores the *Noronic*'s
uncharred decks by replacing flame with mist.

No task's too small or too massive for *here*
whether it's scraping a century's grime
from stone-turreted St Luke's United
or clearing Jarvis Street of the concrete
megaliths layered over flophouses
to reveal chestnut walks and mansard roofs.

It's the peopled streetscapes that pose the most
daunting challenge for *you* to roll aside
the stones of years and reach the unwrinkled
inhabitants of *here* still strolling down
those still unpaved streets and enter the
wished-for world of their shiny afterlife.

We'll never hear the escaped slaves
who gathered in the British Methodist
   Episcopalian Church to sing
Now Let Me Fly lauding Ezekiel's wheels
   like the Underground Railroad wheels
that rolled them to Toronto and freedom

   now that the church has flown away
like wingborne song just as the Hippodrome
   where Sophie Tucker warbled out
praise to her Yiddishe Momme is dust
   particles underneath the square
beneath our city hall's circular wings

   no more than we can hear any
of the fifteen Glionna children all
   musical sweetening the air
of the Glionna Hotel with their songs
   unless their music has infused
the drills of the Dentistry Faculty

   that has replaced the Glionna
or perhaps it still hovers in the air
   awaiting some keen-eared creatures
that have yet to evolve and can decode
   old chantings the way a laser
decodes CDs or the way a dog's nose

can read the air's timeworn scent-trails
and sense a kinship with what has vanished
  but until such beings appear
we must rely on imagination
  which has always been first cousin
to the listening ear of empathy.

THE SWIMMING HOLE

To swim is also to take hold
On water's meaning.

Charles Tomlinson

was a work of the imagination
blotting out smoke's traces from riverside
chimneys in the background or the foreground's
flotsam of sewage browning the current

a fable aided by photographers
unmanning the manhood of the swimmers
transforming them to classical statues
by a cheeky focus fixed behind them

yet to be swimmer rather than viewer
put body in imagination's work
being supported by this translucent
element that slipped through a grasping hand

leaving the nineteenth century's belief
in solid substance matter for debate
as you became a bird or an angel
winging your way through thin reflected clouds

naked as on the morning you were born
into pinched poverty and now reborn
into a floating world rebaptized whole
with waters from the river's streaming silk

VI

Today the clouds are offering
free tutorials in melting
the wind shooting invisible
cannonballs at them drilling blue
circles into the centre of
every lace-fringed cumulus puff

which the wind then nibbles away
from the inside outwards the way
this child sitting at Tim Hortons
on Yonge a few stores north of Bloor
tackles his donut widening
a hole inside the white-iced ring.

It's always been a holey place
since the *Courier* complained
in eighteen thirty-three about
"that chain of mudholes called Yonge Street"
and now the asphalt roadbed groans
where cars run this year's pothole chains

while blocks away if you listen
above ironclad maintenance-
holes you can catch the burbling talk
of what is left of Taddle Creek
as it roams the lakeward slope
along an O of sewer pipe

and several blocks the other way
among spruce lining the ravine
three O-gape mouths crane from the small
donut-shaped nest a cardinal –
to shield it from the wind's barrage –
has anchored in an arc of branch.

EVOLUTION AT THE BRICK WORKS

I

Think layer cake and think of human thought
as a thin glaze poured over the icing
which itself is layered from the topmost
Sunnybrook Drift fifty thousand years old
down to the York Till spread on bedrock one
hundred thirty-five thousand years ago

by a master glacier whose patient art
practiced by succeeding generations
spreading and scraping spreading and scraping
dropped clues to each age the Don Formation
working in a warmer kitchen leaving
fossil traces later found farther south

from Papaw Blue Ash Shagbark Hickory
to White Cedar while the Scarborough chef
sweatered against a Boreal climate
used his culinary skills to fashion
Sugar Maple Oak and other species
whose leaves still heap up on our autumn paths.

2

Think in minutes and seconds to measure
evolution's next step at the Brick Works
not the unimaginable expanse
traversed by stone over lifeless aeons
but inches sunk by William Taylor's boot
as it drives a shovel into the clay

and microscopic distances his brain's
synapses bridge as his thoughts fire the clay
of 1882 into the bricks
of 1889 with seven shades
of buff green-gold and brown obsidian
emerging when mixed with Mud Creek's waters

to raise the walls of Convocation Hall
and half the houses around it the Brick Works'
own buildings swept away like glacial till
when William's latest brainstorms made old ones
seem like fossils embedded in a rock
not of ages but of our mortal hours.

3

Think restoration of a landscape that
was never really there and think what thought
can do since what is real will always be
a gift sent by the imagination
a quilt spread over thoughtless layerings
of time as over a hollow quarry

once heaped with stone deposited by earth's
long restless mindless sleep and then scooped out
by hands and minds alive to ice and fire
the ice of glacial clay that turned sun-bright
when fired in a kiln the sky-blue shale
transformed by the kiln to ten shades of red

where now the empty quarry fructifies
as resurrected waters from the once-
buried Mud Creek filter like glacial melt
through lily-freshed ponds to freshen the Don
feeding bergamot aster primrose that
thoughtful hands have planted along the way.

She sees with her fingers like the blind
fingering braille although not blind just
so extremely sensitive to light

she wears a dark mask around her eyes
to ward off glare and is always most
awake at night when she ventures out

to get food for her young family
whom she protects with claw and bared fang
and who have inherited her sense

of touch equipped from an early age
to unscrew jar lids uncork bottles
lift gate latches and open hinged bins

before returning to the lean-to
behind the garage where they bed down
in and among our stored snow tires

an immigrant family though their
ancestors lived here thousands of years
before brick walls displaced hollow trees

and cars reduced the species' lifespan
leaving her to rub her fine hands and
look the picture of anxiety.

TRICKS ON THE HUMBER
(HURRICANE HAZEL)

Was it the water god – come back after
two hundred years of disbelief – who hung
the few remaining elms with hockey sticks

dolls umbrellas and – from the rubber works
upriver – rain-fattened prophylactics
or was this uproar beyond the powers

of a lone god no impetuous breach
of bounds but a long-premeditated
conspiracy of water with the wind

that ripped up roadway stop signs hurling them
like spears and brandished roofing tiles like blades
slashing through walls and windows of houses

along the floodplain this pair of tricksters
who – knowing nothing of mortality –
upended grazing cattle and turned swing-

bridges into diving boards for drivers
lost in a pouring dark the forecasters
were tricked into calling "occasional

light rain" as the one-time Carrying Place
for canoes carried bankside bungalows
down to the lake
                        but now where their streets ran

treed pathways line the floodplain though sometimes
the odd pedal pokes through the grass as if
some trickster rode a bike into the ground.

GONE

When Sugar Loaf Hill was carted off
as fill for the Don Valley Parkway

    a house dubbed *Drumsnab* (northern word for
    sugar loaf) lost its why and wherefore

        the steel-clad viaduct no longer
        sharing heights with a tree-clad neighbour.

Down on the valley floor the meadow's
bare ground was widowed of its shadow

    missing the hill's ample umbrella
    picnickers twirled flimsy parasols

        over the site of the swimming hole
        whose mouth was now plugged with hill-rubble.

Butternut ash maple and walnut
dwindled into timber and firewood

    climbing raccoons no more sipped sweetness
    from trunks of the Sugar Loaf's bee trees

        phoebe and swallow left bereft of
        the winged future dormant in their nests.

MEMORIAL QUILT,
YORK MILLS SUBWAY STATION

All five kneel but only two are praying
in a quilt sewn by Laurie Swim that hangs
underground in the subway station's hall

metres from a water main tunnel where
the five construction workers lost their lives
when toxic smoke snaked into their workplace.

All five kneel because no one could stand up
underneath the cramped tunnel's low ceiling
the brothers Guido and Alessandro

pressed knee to knee and hand to praying hand
wombed once more in Mother Earth while the three
others might be paying homage to light

that seems to pour from a brilliant white sun
of unfinished cloth at this tunnel's end
though the bricked tunnel veiled them in darkness.

The quilt translates rock's hardness into cloth
and pinks the dried-blood-red bricks to pastels
strewing the ground with patches of blossom

as in a funeral's spray of flowers
reminding us so softly that we are
also made of perishable fabric.

LOCAL GHOSTS

Never trust the teller, trust the tale.

D.H. Lawrence

I

Never trust the teller or the tale in lurid
tales like that of Dorothy a bank teller who
shot herself in the head with the bank's revolver
after a failed affair with another teller
and switches lights on and off and trips buzzers in
the building that became the Hockey Hall of Fame

or tales of how Arthur Lucas and Ron Turpin
the last murderers in Canada to be hanged
escape from holding places in old City Hall
and fling writs from the tops of filing cabinets
tugging at the judges' black robes to catch them up
and scaling stairways to climb to ghostly freedom

or of course the saga of Ivan Reznikoff
University College's master carver
whose mournful gargoyle face peeks out from the ivy
near where he chased his rival with an axe but was
himself stabbed and thrown into a stairwell where he
waylays midnight visitors with his sad story.

No murderer's ghost haunts the Robarts Library
"Fort Book" being ghastly enough without such ghosts
a concrete castle in the style of Franz Kafka
dwarfing students cowering under its towers
the Robarts' ghosts are domestic apparitions
vestiges of Victorian homes on its site

memories that lost their anchorage when houses
were demolished like the sloping floorboards that held
the sounds of children giggling as their roller skates
swept them from one end of the house to the other
or the third-floor window glass that flung leaf patterns
floorwards from the maple turning room to tree-house

or the honeycomb of mouse holes tunneling through
the basement joists underneath the kitchen where what
she thought was one wee lonely mouse though its fur
    seemed
to change colour in shifting lights was kept alive
by frequent offerings of dinner leftovers
from a stooped old woman whose name it's said was
    Grace.

VII

THE MAKING OF AN ARCHITECT

In the treehouse I learned a lot about
unstructured learning.

Raymond Moriyama

And a lot about inclusion after
being excluded by a colony
of WASPS who drove off you and twenty-two
thousand others for being Japanese

a sting compounded in the shower room
when playmates teased you as *diseased* because
your back was scarred from an old injury
so you decamped and bathed in solitude

in the Slocan River's frigid waters
building a sentry post in an old tree
where you could see intruders from far off
and where forest and mountainside began

unstructured lessons in nature-watching
the simple wooden platform your first work
of architecture and fit training-ground
for the boy who would grow up to dream up

a hands-on Science Centre balanced on
the side of a ravine and inspired by
an adage of Confucius *when you hear*
you forget when you see you remember

some but when you touch and do it becomes
part of you as the trees and site contours
you preserved are your mind's forest sloping
down the valley to your heart's watercourse

and as the banked tiers of your Library
overflowing with plants open around
the central atrium in welcome like
blossoming flowers or unfolding arms.

REVELL'S CITY HALL

*Speak, that I may see thee … [speech] springs
out of the most retired and inward part of us.*

Ben Jonson

Statement is structure
thought has taken form
   and poured itself out in words

the liquid mixture
on contact with air
   solidifying to stone

and as speech carries
accents embossed by
   the speaker's lips tongue and teeth

concrete shows traces
of its origins
   the aggregate's size and shape

texture of the frame
in which it was cast
   be it nubbed like raw lumber

or silk-smooth as steel
the ribbed tower walls
   and the glazed inner facade

their architect as
sculptor fashioning
    this nest between the spread wings

of parent birds this
home for speech where speech
    has been transformed into song.

The glacier's chisel and the drills
of running water grooved ravines
into this earth but our mountains
needed help from human hands to
raise themselves and our rootbound gaze.

Limestone and sandstone long buried
on the escarpment rose once more
to flesh out steel-beamed skeletons
while silica from dried-up shores
melted to glaze light's apertures

where human eyes like unhooded
peregrines no longer confined
to nearness could like those falcons
soar beyond barricading trees.
Yet distances of space whispered

the same song distances of time
had printed into the limestone
where crinoid fossils' rounded mouths
hold star-shaped tongues that tell of long
reaches beyond our human hands.

MYSTERIES OF AN URBAN MOUNTAIN

*Her own consciousness is only one among an infinite
number of focal points on and in the mountain.*

> Robert Macfarlane
> on Nan Shepherd's *The Living Mountain*

She never looks twice into the same sky
clouds like animated puzzle pieces
shifting positions and no position
more right than others in an abstract art
that refuses to depict a landscape

sky a mirror of the streets beneath it
where tiny rectangles of cars and trucks
scuttle like icons in a vast board game
while dots of people wait at traffic lights
and move in clusters as if magnetized

a scale the looker rejects when she leaves
for the elevator like a climber
rappelling down a mountain rock face and
looking up from her valley floor becomes
suddenly humbled by the sheernesses

and realizes her view "only one
among an infinite number" of views
from the building's hundreds of apartments
her apartment changing to a withment
in a landscape of living mysteries.

REALMS OF GOLD

For Hugh Anson-Cartwright, bookseller

ten levels tall but containing
hundreds of storied apartments
the gold not merely embossed on
nameplates of leather-covered doors

but dispersed in the air breathed by
the occupants who inhaling
its pure serene grow immortal
some of them thousands of years old

each apartment detachable
from adjacent units opens
doors to rooms whose seeming flatness
deepens as you walk into them

on guard against blasts of snowsqualls
from some explorer's hoary hall
but welcoming a burble of
song from the saxophone whose notes

spill from the margins of a door
imprinted with Czech lettering
like the squiggled northern islands
on one of David Thompson's maps

in a neighbouring apartment
or the arcs and oblique angles
of a Wyndham Lewis drawing
installed on an upper level

from which the gathered company
glimpses a genial concierge
welcoming visitors to this
house of golden conversations.

THE WANDERING ISLANDS

We owe them to the Niagara River
whose currents snaking across Lake Ontario
  ate away the clays of Scarborough Bluffs
creating sandbars like a row of parapets

  guarding the inner harbour time would carve
but long before the land knew itself as harbour
  the sandbars greened with grasses shrubs and trees
and became places of healing and vision-quest

  for the Mississaugas whose spirits sensed
unearthly companionship where mists and low clouds
  blurred one island's banks into another's
and what early eyes did with islands later tongues

  have done with island names Centre Island's
dock in fact on Middle Island not on Centre
  while Centre Island's eastern end is called
Ward's Island and the waterway of Hanlan's Bay

  has been buried under Bishop runways
by the same dredging that raised the Island Airport
  with Algonquin Island formerly known
as Sunfish Island sometime before Jim Crow Pond

  was filled in by South Island to the east
of Long Pond referred to in the 1890s
  as Kennedy Pond containing a small
shrub-covered island at times called Duckling Island

south of Middle Island whose rides in its
amusement park not to be confused with the one
once on Hanlan's Island may induce a
dizziness like being lost among the islands.

TWO BOATMEN

Threads of their lives crisscrossing the Island
in its tapestry of Hanlans and Wards
(Ned's sunny yellow, William's midnight black)
they must have met even before Ned's first
rowing competition when William's boat
emerged a winner and Ned's failed to place –

an order the following years reversed
as Ned left other rowers in his wake
toying with opponents letting them al-
most catch up resting on his oars before
shooting ahead to grinning victory
while bands played "See the Conquering Hero"

that tune remote from William's troubled thoughts
as he gave up racing for lifesaving
to undo what could never be undone
and rescue the five sisters who had drowned
when he at fifteen took them in his boat
for an afternoon cruise across the bay

where wind catching the sail capsized the craft
and spilled non-swimmers Rose, Jane, Cecilia,
Phoebe, and Mary Ann – weighed down by white
Sunday pinafores – under white-trimmed waves
that towered every night in William's dreams
even after he saved the *Jane Ann Marsh*

sailors from a frozen death by making
seven trips across the icy waters
or later when a revived man's first words
called for the "poor girl, poor girl" who had been
his love but never became one of the
hundred and forty-six William rescued

before he died in 1912 four years
after Ned Hanlan fourteen years before
the city honoured its famous boatman
with a heroic bronze statue of Ned
who stands arm round a raised oar like a spear
beside the ferry dock at Hanlan's Point.

VIII

I

hunkered on this resting-place for rubble
looking lakewards at blue infinity
it's easy to slide into the deep past

bricks and mortar half-submerged in a stretch
of wall fused and rounded by the caress
of waves dissolve into Pleistocene clay

twisted rebar-loops crane skeletal necks
from concrete nests and spread Pterodactyl
wings skyward in frozen mating dances

hard to believe the weight of sediment
dredged from the harbour and pressed down by spoil
from subway excavation pressed further

by demolition detritus subsoil
and bedrock would not compress to the shale
sunk beneath Pangaea's ancient seabed

or is this a distant future prospect
a landmass as devoid of people as
the sunlit-rippled surface that supports

no streets no street traffic no traffic lights
or engine noise only redwing blackbirds'
o-ka-la-leee and the see-mee see-mee

of black-capped chickadees unseen by us
in branches of sandbar willows where seeds
root themselves without aid of human hands

where showy lady's slipper flourishes
in the absence of ladies and slippers
our help unneeded by white sweet clover

whose roots releasing nitrogen enrich
soil purged of our phosphates by an age as
free of human pressures as Pangaea

SECOND THOUGHTS ON THE
LESLIE STREET SPIT

I come into the peace of wild things
who do not tax their lives with forethought
of grief.
>Wendell Berry

They're sometimes not so peaceful let's leave
aside wild things like the zombie wasp
that stings a roach and then seals an egg

in the zombified roach's belly
where the wasp larva grows and feeds on
the belly and the rest of the roach

or the cordyceps fungus blooming
from an infected ant's head to spread
spores that contaminate further hosts

and let's stick to wild things on this spit
of wilderness dangling like a fob
from the city beside the harbour

where forethought of grief though it cannot
prevent a bird-brained flycatcher from
neglecting her own brood to mother

the cowbird smuggled into her nest
can build reef-raft nests for cormorants
to keep them from the cottonwood trees

their droppings would destroy and can hang
fish gates to maintain threatened small fry
barring the carp that would savage them

and forethought of grief protects tender
aquatic plantlife from predation
by the seven-foot-tall Phragmites

controlling with other herbicides
the Dog-Strangling Vine that masquerades
as milkweed but offers no relief

to the monarch butterfly's efforts
when she pauses her peaceful journey
and trusts her eggs to a milkweed's care.

After the torchlit fishing parties at
the river's mouth with salmon so profuse
they wove a silver path from the canoes
at midstream to the marshy shoreline where
herons and egrets nested in thick reeds

After the last moccasin left its print
on the shoals of rotting sawdust drifted
down from the mill upriver clotting with
the tannery's lime the lye from soapworks
and carcasses from the slaughterhouses

After the last salmon speared at Taylor's
paper mill in 1874
left unaccompanied by elegies
from warblers curlews and sandpipers who
followed exiting herons and egrets

- - - - - -

There came runoff from the river's lesser
tributaries sewer systems that sluiced
gutter waste animal offal manure
into the vanishing fish spawning grounds
of a current being choked to stillness

There came landfill stopping up the wetlands
the largest coastal marsh in the Great Lakes
sinking under the weight of dredged-up silt
building rubble garbage trucked in to make
refined neighbourhoods for oil storage tanks

There came influx of earth-moving machines
to make the water follow a straight line
as if rivers could turn at right angles
in defiance of the paths of nature
and when they didn't in flowed floodwaters

- - - - - -

And now the river valley rings once more
with clinking shovels small ones nurturing
seedlings feeding them topsoil and large ones
making up a more comfortable bed
for the river's meandering body

And now where birds fled new breeding grounds grow
along the river mouth's restored wetlands
the air flooding with *sweet*-songed chickadees
indigo buntings kildeer tree swallows
the water swishing with returned salmon

And now children will weave branches to build
castles along the park's aspen-lined paths
and grow into adults whose limbs know well
that the ground under their feet is a weave
of riverbank and imagination

"Moss Park, the Hon. William Allan House": Title
and quoted lines are from William Dendy, *Lost Toronto*
(Toronto: McClelland & Stewart, 1993).

"Boxed": Henry "Box" Brown and Ann O'Rourke lived
in Corktown on Toronto's lower east side.

"The Making of a Clown": The Skelton epigraph is
quoted by Michael Posner in *The Ward*, edited by John
Lorinc, Michael McClelland, and Ellen Scheinberg
(Toronto: Coach House Books, 2015).

"Heaven on Elizabeth Street": The site of the Elizabeth
Street playground is now occupied by the eastern wing
of the Sick Children's Hospital.

"At the Red Lion": See Matt. 27:7–8, where the chief
priest took Judas's thirty pieces of silver "and bought with
them the potter's field, to bury strangers in. Wherefore
that field was called The field of blood."

"The Swimming Hole": Epigraph is from Charles
Tomlinson, "Swimming Chenango Lake," *Collected
Poems* (Oxford: Oxford University Press, 1987).

"Mysteries of an Urban Mountain": Epigraph is from
Robert Macfarlane's introduction to Nan Shepherd's *The
Living Mountain* (Edinburgh: Canongate Books, 2011).

"Second Thoughts on the Leslie Street Spit": Epigraph is from Wendell Berry, *The Peace of Wild Things and Other Poems* (London: Penguin Books, 2018).

Toronto is fortunate in having many accomplished chroniclers of its people and places, and I have benefited especially from the information and the stories found in: Eric Arthur, *Toronto: No Mean City*, 3rd ed., revised by Stephen A. Otto (Toronto: University of Toronto Press, 2003); Dale Barbour, *Undressed Toronto* (Winnipeg: University of Manitoba Press, 2023); G.P. de T. Glazebrook, *The Story of Toronto* (Toronto: University of Toronto Press, 1971); Walter H. Kehm, *Accidental Wilderness* (University of Toronto Press, 2020); Allan Levine, *Toronto: Biography of a City* (Vancouver: Douglas & McIntyre, 2014); John Lorinc, Michael McClelland, and Ellen Scheinberg, eds., *The Ward* (Toronto: Coach House Books, 2015); Don Loucks and Leslie Valpy, *Modest Hopes* (Toronto: Dundern Press, 2021); Holly Martelle, Michael McClelland, Tatum Taylor, and John Lorinc, eds., *The Ward Uncovered* (Toronto: Coach House Books, 2018); Shawn Micallef, *Stroll* (Toronto: Coach House Books, 2010); Edward S. Rogers and Donald B. Smith, eds., *Aboriginal Ontario* (Toronto: Dundern Press, 1994); and Charles Sauriol, *Remembering the Don* (Toronto: Consolidated Amethyst Communications, 1981), and *Tales of the Don* (Toronto: Natural Heritage/Natural History, 1984).

Some of these poems have appeared in *Canadian Literature*, *The Fiddlehead*, *grain*, and *Poems for a Birthday*, ed. David Kent (Toronto: St Thomas Poetry Series, 2020). I am grateful to the editors for their encouragement. Further encouragement has come from my fellow poets in the Vic Group, this time especially from Ariane Blackman, Sue Chenette, Maureen Hynes, Marvyne Jenoff, and K.D. Miller. At MQUP, I am once again indebted to my editor, Allan Hepburn, for his kindness and his keen eye.

Some of these poems may appeared in *Canadian Literature*, *The Malahat Review*, and *Prairie Fire*. *Raise the roof* (2010), Kerry Prestina, St. Thomas Poetry Series, 2010. I am grateful to the editors for their encouragement. Further thanks go to the poet from many poetry peers in the Vic Centre, this remarkable group: Arthur, Bergman, Sue Chenoa, Maureen Hynes, Marvin Francis, Ken D. Miller, A. Wright. I am once again indebted to my editor, Allan Stephens, for his kindness and his keen eye.